The poems in this book are meant to spread awareness and encourage discussions with children about the world we live in, the problems we face, and how to resolve them. They were inspired by the Global Goals for Sustainable Development which were established by 193 world leaders at the United Nations Sustainable Development Summit in the General Assembly in New York, 2015.

The 17 Global Goals are designed to help achieve three objectives: (1) End extreme poverty, (2) Fight inequality and injustice, (3) Fix climate change. They are meant to be implemented by citizens and governments worldwide to ensure achievement of these goals by the year 2030.

In 2030, the children who read this book will be at a prime age to participate in the society that we are preparing for them. Let us educate them so they will be willing and able to take positive action in the world.

Enjoy! *Holly Olsen*

Nursery Rhymes for Social Good

Alternative poems for future activists.

For Olivia, Ruby, Sonoma & Estee

Written by Holly Olsen

Illustrated by Elie Galih

Star light, star bright,
Wishing's not enough tonight.
I'll speak up, work, or walk all night,
Until what's wrong is changed to right.

Little Bo Peep is losing her sleep.
She can't afford to live well.
It's oft' not enough to work 'n be tough.
That's a myth that we all must dispel.

If giv'n a chance, she can advance.
Please let her buy some land.
With options and rights and access to lights,
On her own two feet, she'll stand.

5

ZERO HUNGER

*"End hunger, achieve food security and improved
nutrition and promote sustainable agriculture"*

Hey, diddle, diddle,
Please spare just a little,
And I'll be over the moon.
There's plenty of food
To lighten the mood,
So let's share with a dish and a spoon!

GOOD HEALTH & WELL-BEING

*"Ensure healthy lives and promote
well-being for all at all ages"*

Eenie, meenie, miney moe,
People need a healthy glow.
If we're healthy, it will show.
Eenie, meenie, miney moe.

4

QUALITY EDUCATION

"Ensure inclusive and equitable quality education and promote lifelong learning opportunities for all"

Baa, baa, bright sheep,
Want to go to school?
Yes, ma'am, yes ma'am
Learning is so cool.
Education opens doors,
It helps you to succeed,
It's something we all long for,
And something we all need.

Baa, baa, bright sheep,
Do not be a fool.
Let's make it happen:
Everyone in school!

5

GENDER EQUALITY

*"Achieve gender equality and empower
all women and girls"*

Snips and snails and puppy dogs' tails,
That's what we're ALL made of –
With sugar and spice and everything nice,
Yes, that's what we're ALL made of!

6

CLEAN WATER & SANITATION

*"Ensure availability and sustainable management
of water and sanitation for all"*

Jack and Jane went down the lane
To fetch a pail of water.
It must be clean and safe to drink,
For every son and daughter!

AFFORDABLE & CLEAN ENERGY

"Ensure access to affordable, reliable, sustainable and modern energy for all"

Twinkle, twinkle, energy,
Power gives us what we need.
Fossil fuels are not the way.
Renewables could save the day!
Twinkle, twinkle, energy,
Power gives us what we need.

DECENT WORK & ECONOMIC GROWTH

"Promote sustained, inclusive and sustainable economic growth, full and productive employment and decent work for all"

Hickory dickory dock,
Good jobs, they mean a lot!
Fair pay, safe way,
Respect, okay,
Hickory, dickory, dock!

9

INDUSTRY, INNOVATION & INFRASTRUCTURE

"Build resilient infrastructure, promote inclusive and sustainable industrialization and foster innovation"

Row, hoe, show your work,
Imagine and create!
Make something new,
Then trade a few.
'Cause industry is great!

10

REDUCED INEQUALITIES

"Reduce inequality within and among countries"

Five little speckled frogs
Sat on a hollow log
Whether they were brown
or green or white.

Fun, fun!

It didn't matter who they were,
The kinds of bugs that they preferred,
Frogs are frogs, and should
have equal rights.

Fun, fun!

SUSTAINABLE CITIES & COMMUNITIES

*"Make cities and human settlements inclusive,
safe, resilient and sustainable"*

Three kind mice. Three kind mice.
See how they live. See how they live.
With safety and comfort
they each have a place,
In cities where they are
all welcomed each day,
We must work together
to keep it that way,
With three kind mice.

RESPONSIBLE CONSUMPTION & PRODUCTION

"Ensure sustainable consumption and production patterns"

There was an old woman
with too many shoes.
She had so many things,
and didn't reuse.

Using up all of the
things in the world,
Will only bring sadness
to each boy and girl.

CLIMATE ACTION

*"Take urgent action to combat
climate change and its impacts"*

Diddle dee - do SOMEthing,
friends, come on.
Clean air and water
make our lives go on.
The earth is getting hot,
so we call upon
All to diddle dee- do SOMEthing,
friends, come on!

LIFE BELOW WATER

"Conserve and sustainably use the oceans, seas and marine resources for sustainable development"

It's raining, it's pouring,
The ocean needs restoring.
I have a dream to keep it clean,
So fish can keep exploring.

LIFE ON LAND

*"Protect, restore and promote sustainable
use of terrestrial ecosystems"*

Humpty Dumpty sat in a nest,
Calling to all,
"Mother Nature knows best!
I'm out on a limb.
Without trees, life is grim.
Let's save them together
and everyone wins!"

PEACE, JUSTICE & STRONG INSTITUTIONS

"Promote peaceful and inclusive societies, provide access to justice for all and build effective, accountable and inclusive institutions"

Little Miss Muffet, sat on a tuffet,
Leaving her food at bay;
She won't take a bite,
Until we don't fight,
And that's all that she wants to say.

PARTNERSHIP FOR THE GOALS

"Strengthen the means of implementation and revitalize the global partnership for sustainable development"

The wheels on the bus
of change go round
Come on down,
Make a sound!
We can make a difference
All around!
Change abound!

ABOUT THE AUTHOR

Holly Olsen lives in Connecticut with her husband and four daughters. She has a masters degree in Second Language Teaching from Utah State University, and a BA in Spanish with a minor in International Studies. She co-founded a bilingual preschool with a focus on social and environmental justice. In recent years, she co-founded the nonprofit HemoHelper where she helps provide medical IDs and supplies to hemophiliacs in developing countries.

THE ORIGINAL NURSERY RHYMES